cole porter

Arranged by Brent Edstrom

contents

2	AT LONG LAST LOVE
8	BEGIN THE BEGUINE
5	DREAM DANCING
14	EASY TO LOVE (YOU'D BE SO EASY TO LOVE)
22	EV'RY TIME WE SAY GOODBYE
17	FROM THIS MOMENT ON
26	GET OUT OF TOWN
30	I CONCENTRATE ON YOU
35	I GET A KICK OUT OF YOU
40	I LOVE PARIS
48	I'VE GOT YOU UNDER MY SKIN
43	IN THE STILL OF THE NIGHT
52	IT'S ALL RIGHT WITH ME
63	IT'S DE-LOVELY
58	JUST ONE OF THOSE THINGS
68	LET'S DO IT (LET'S FALL IN LOVE)
74	LOVE FOR SALE
71	MY HEART BELONGS TO DADDY
80	NIGHT AND DAY
84	WHAT IS THIS THING CALLED LOVE?
88	YOU DO SOMETHING TO ME
92	YOU'D BE SO NICE TO COME HOME TO

Cover photo © Sasha/Getty Images

ISBN 978-1-4803-6236-9

Visit Hal Leonard Online at
www.halleonard.com

Contact us:
Hal Leonard
7777 West Bluemound Road
Milwaukee, WI 53213
Email: info@halleonard.com

In Europe, contact:
Hal Leonard Europe Limited
42 Wigmore Street
Marylebone, London, W1U 2RN
Email: info@halleonardeurope.com

In Australia, contact:
Hal Leonard Australia Pty. Ltd.
4 Lentara Court
Cheltenham, Victoria, 3192 Australia
Email: info@halleonard.com.au

AT LONG LAST LOVE
from YOU NEVER KNOW

Words and Music by
COLE PORTER

DREAM DANCING

Words and Music by
COLE PORTER

BEGIN THE BEGUINE

from JUBILEE

Words and Music by
COLE PORTER

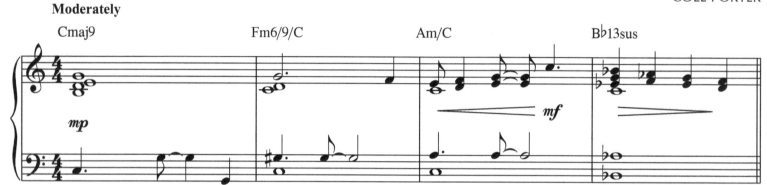

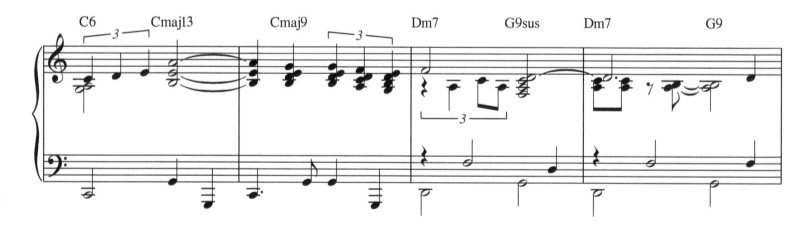

EASY TO LOVE
(You'd Be So Easy to Love)
from BORN TO DANCE

Words and Music by
COLE PORTER

FROM THIS MOMENT ON
from OUT OF THIS WORLD

Words and Music by
COLE PORTER

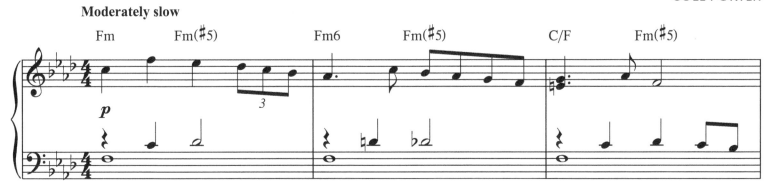

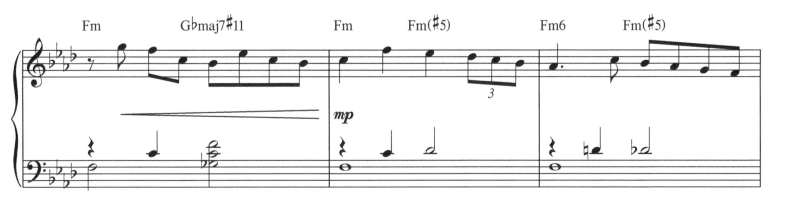

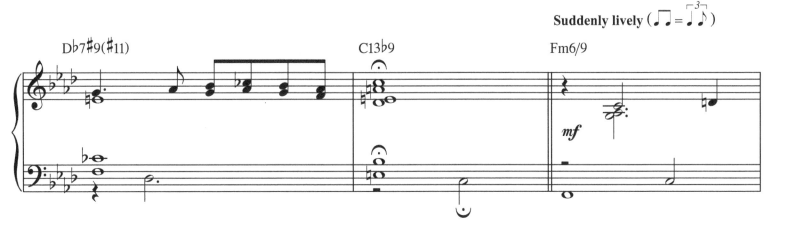

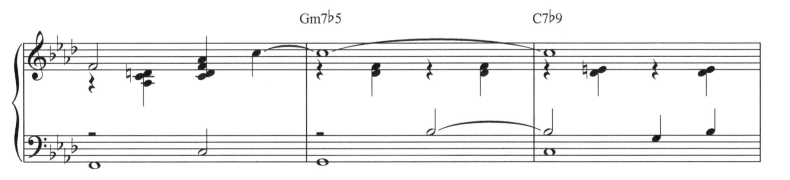

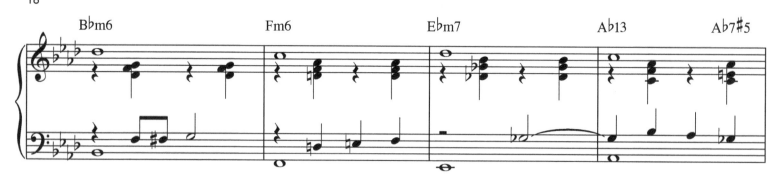

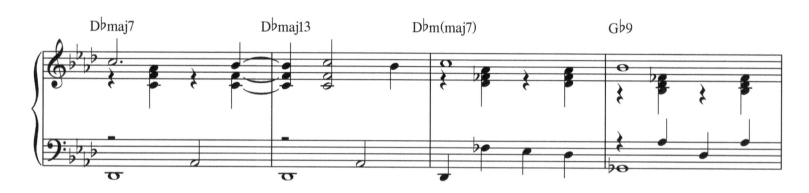

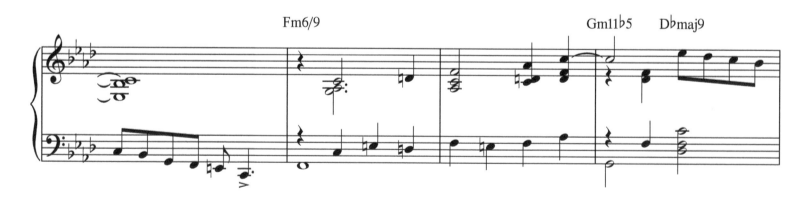

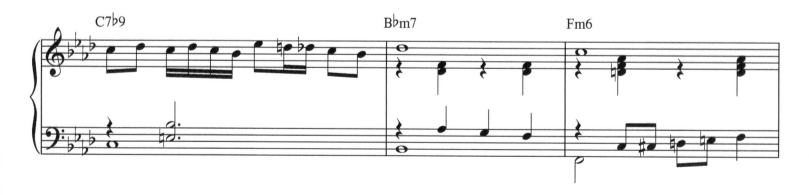

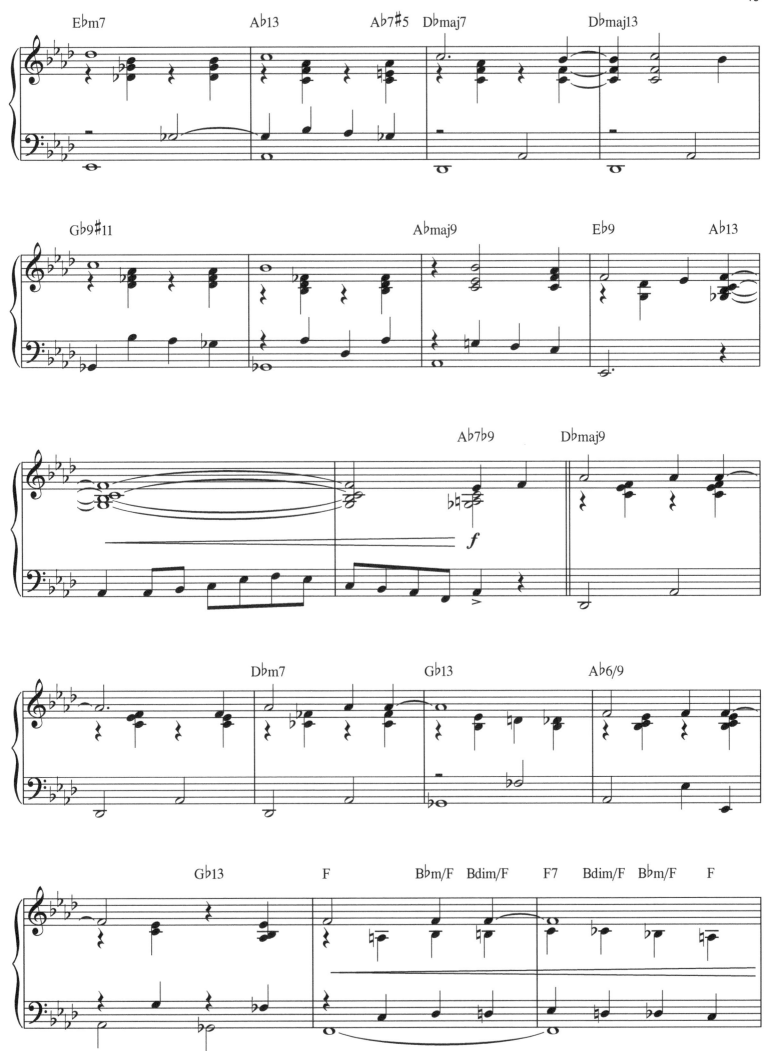

EV'RY TIME WE SAY GOODBYE
from SEVEN LIVELY ARTS

Words and Music by
COLE PORTER

Ballad, with rubato

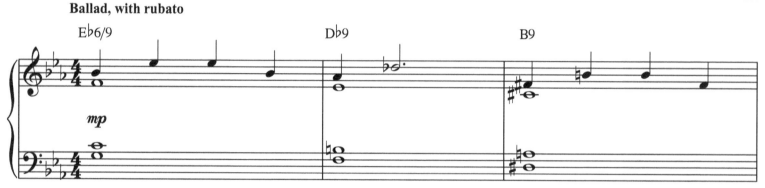

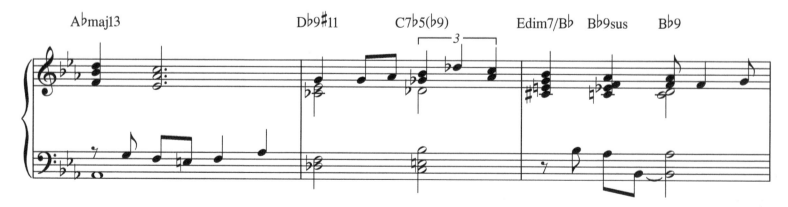

Steady ballad tempo

GET OUT OF TOWN

from LEAVE IT TO ME

Words and Music by
COLE PORTER

Moderately

Freely, with rubato

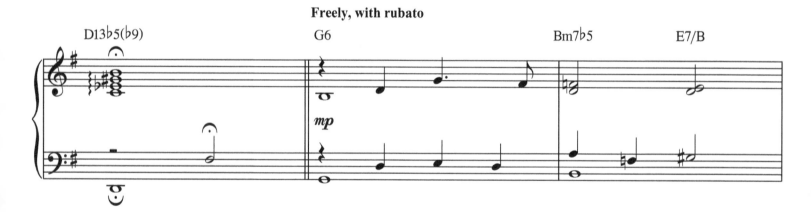

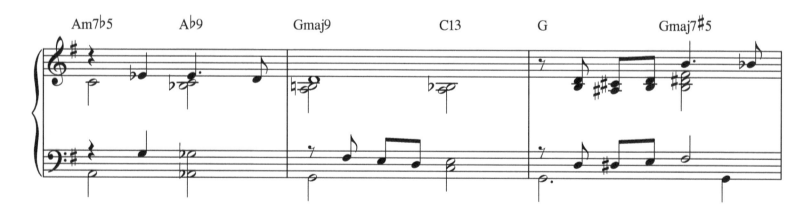

I CONCENTRATE ON YOU
from BROADWAY MELODY OF 1940

Words and Music by
COLE PORTER

I GET A KICK OUT OF YOU
from ANYTHING GOES

Words and Music by
COLE PORTER

Bright Swing

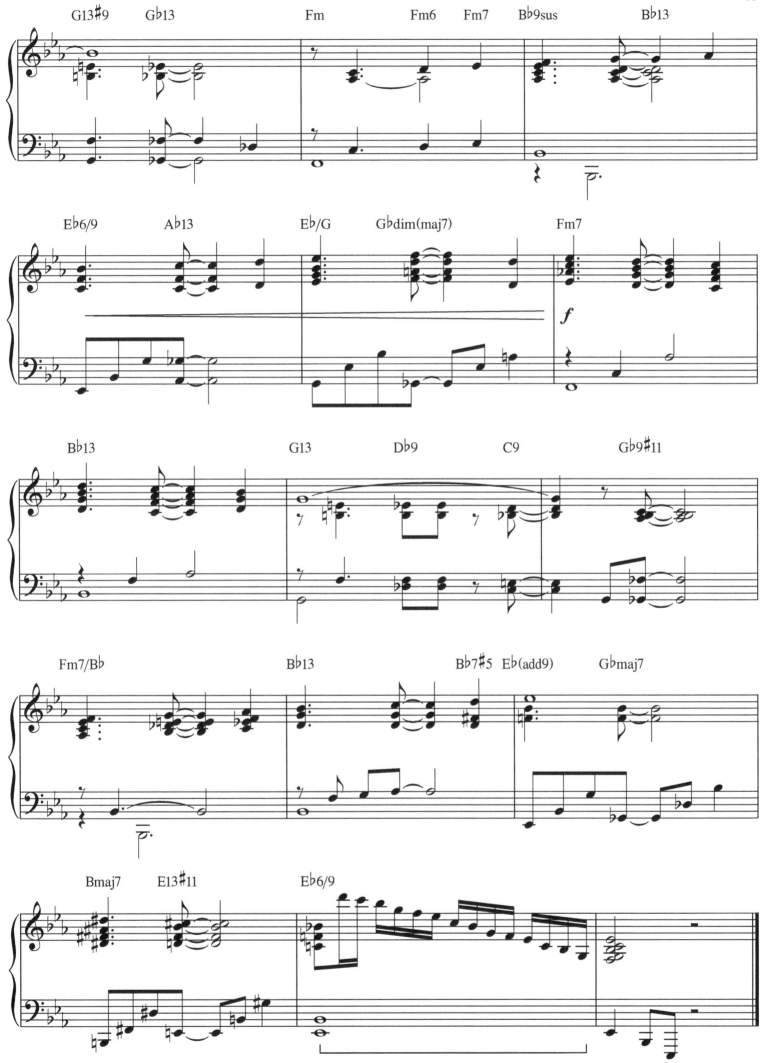

I LOVE PARIS
from CAN-CAN

Words and Music by
COLE PORTER

Moderately, with a humorous undertone

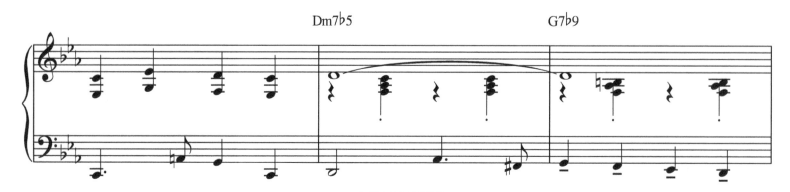

IN THE STILL OF THE NIGHT

from ROSALIE

Words and Music by
COLE PORTER

Medium Swing, mysteriously

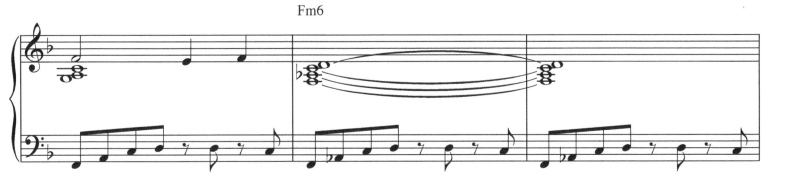

I'VE GOT YOU UNDER MY SKIN
from BORN TO DANCE

Words and Music by
COLE PORTER

IT'S ALL RIGHT WITH ME

from CAN-CAN

Words and Music by
COLE PORTER

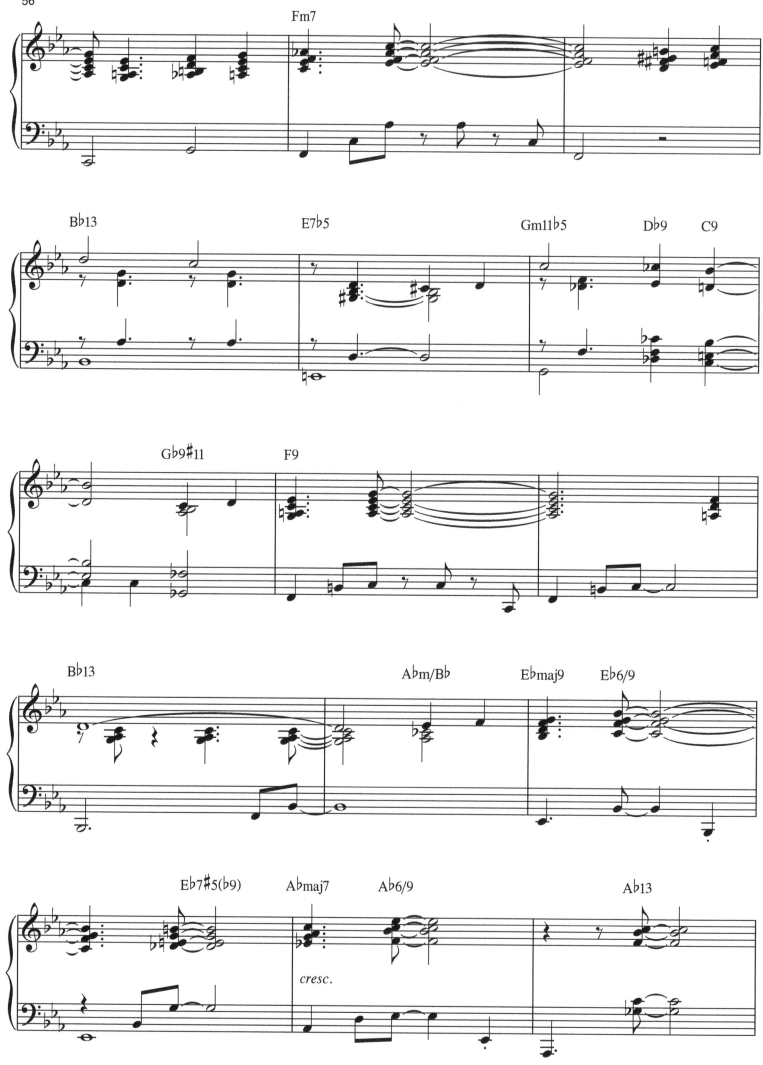

JUST ONE OF THOSE THINGS
from HIGH SOCIETY

Words and Music by
COLE PORTER

IT'S DE-LOVELY
from RED, HOT and BLUE!

Words and Music by
COLE PORTER

LET'S DO IT
(Let's Fall in Love)
from PARIS

Words and Music by
COLE PORTER

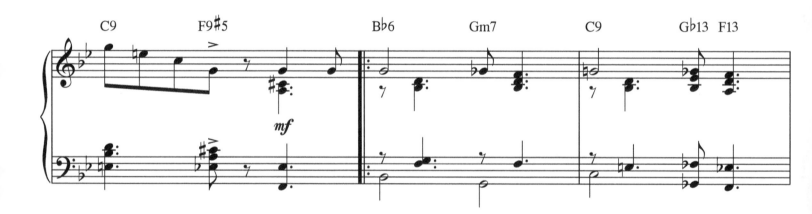

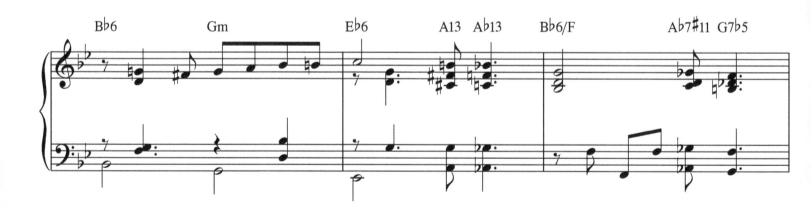

MY HEART BELONGS TO DADDY
from LEAVE IT TO ME

Words and Music by
COLE PORTER

LOVE FOR SALE
from THE NEW YORKERS

Words and Music by
COLE PORTER

Moderate Latin groove

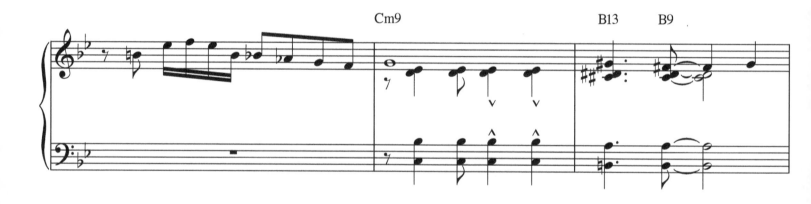

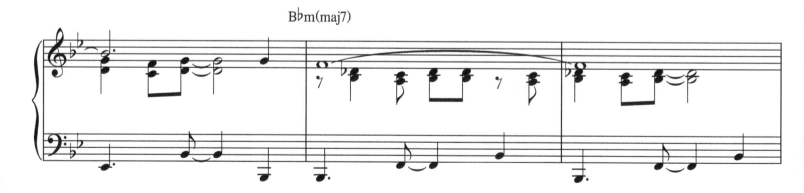

NIGHT AND DAY
from GAY DIVORCE

Words and Music by
COLE PORTER

WHAT IS THIS THING CALLED LOVE?

from WAKE UP AND DREAM

Words and Music by
COLE PORTER

Fast Swing

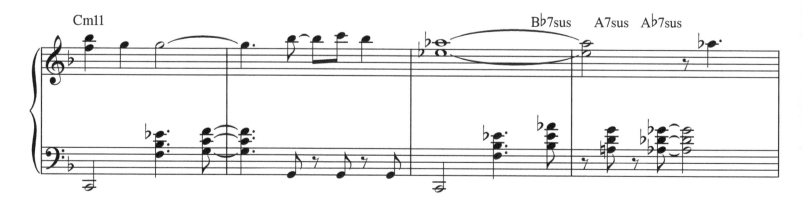

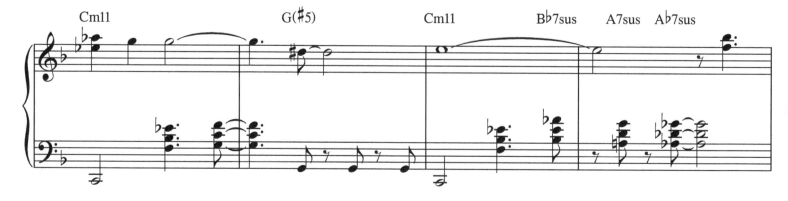

YOU DO SOMETHING TO ME

from CAN-CAN

Words and Music by
COLE PORTER

YOU'D BE SO NICE TO COME HOME TO
from SOMETHING TO SHOUT ABOUT

Words and Music by
COLE PORTER

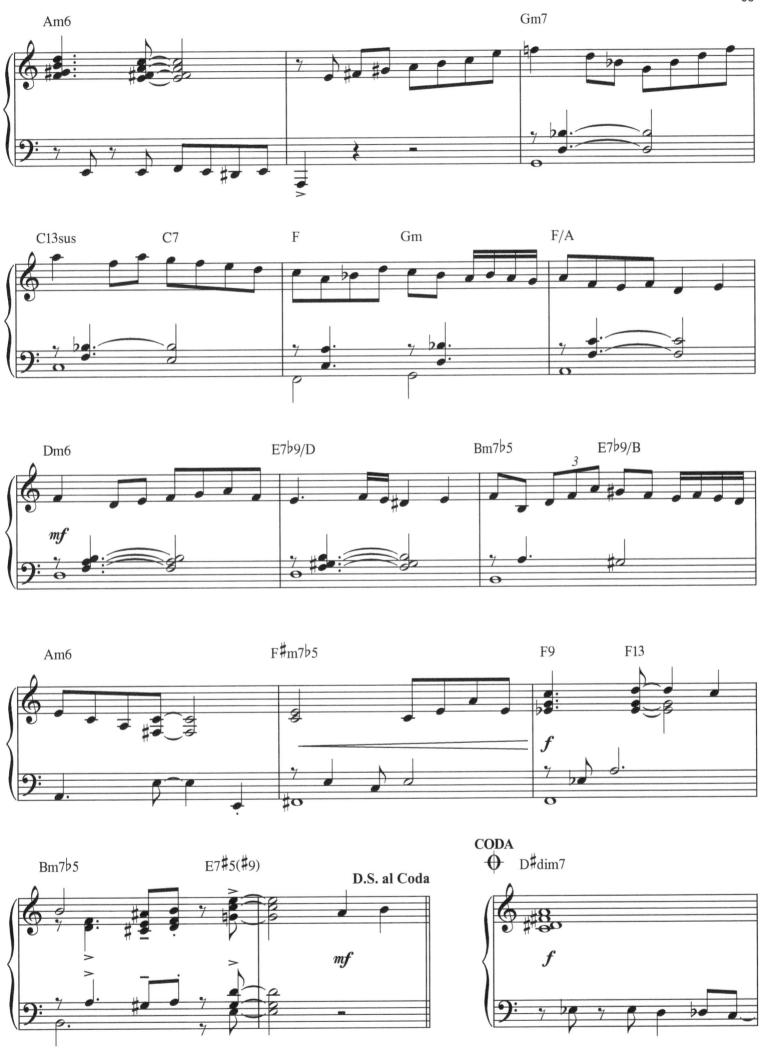